CW00430433

Newmarket

Town & Turf

A Pictorial Tour

Front Cover: Arriving by road from London or Cambridge the visitor cannot fail to notice this impressive statue of The Newmarket Stallion created by Marcia Astor and Allan Sly. It stands high on the roundabout close to the July Racecourse entrance, about two miles from the centre of the town. It was installed there in October 2000.

Back Cover: King Edward VII Memorial Gardens.

© John Worrall and Rodney Vincent 2002
First published 2002

All rights reserved. No part of this publication may be reproduced, in any form or by any means, without the prior consent of the authors.

ISBN   1 904136 05 2

Published by
John Nickalls Publications.
Oak Farm Bungalow, Suton, Wymondham, Norfolk, NR18 9SH.

Printed by
Geo. R. Reeve Ltd., 9-11 Town Green, Wymondham, Norfolk, NR18 0BD.

ACKNOWLEDGEMENTS

The authors and publishers gratefully acknowledge the assistance of The Newmarket Local History Society, the Curator of the National Horseracing Museum and the manager of the Rutland Arms Hotel in providing historical information used in some of the captions to pictures.

Biography: John Worrall
After 15 or 20 years chartered surveying in London, Sydney and Weston-s-Mare, (not necessarily in that order) he saw that life was too short and, in the mid '80s, turned to scribbling and snapping because it was more fun. He settled in East Anglia on which his word processor and camera now tend to concentrate although he is easily lured further afield if a subject is sufficiently interesting. He lives, with Julie, George and Phoebe, in north Norfolk from where he contributes photographs and illustrated features to a range of publications on a mix of landscape, heritage and environmental topics.
His photolibrary (www.anglianimages.co.uk) has extensive medium format coverage of Norfolk, Suffolk and Cambridgeshire together with some adjacent areas and selected subjects in other parts of the country.

He is the author/photographer of two books, East Anglia in Colour (1996, reprinted 2000 and 2001) and East Anglia Through The Seasons (2002), both published by Ian Allan/Dial House.

Biography: Rodney Vincent.
Having spent most of his working life in the gas industry Rodney Vincent retired in 1988 when an Area Manager for British Gas and returned to East Cambridgeshire where he had grown up. He and his wife Audrey now live in the small village of Stuntney. "It's nice and quiet here", he says, "and it's on the Newmarket side of Ely". Newmarket and the surrounding villages have always held a particular interest for him as they bring back so many early memories. He has written about the village of Wood Ditton in his self-published book 'A Tanner Will Do'.
Rodney is the recorder for the Newmarket Local History Society and runs an internet webpage (www.wood-ditton.org.uk/newmarketlhs.htm) for the Society as part of the Wood Ditton site.

Wildlife, the environment and photography have always been particular interests and he is very well aware of the beneficial influence that the Jockey Club, the owners, trainers and the whole of the racing industry have on the countryside.
He is particularly pleased that Newmarket has kept its identity in an age when many towns have been so swamped by development as to become almost unrecognisable.

FOREWORD

Mention the name Newmarket and most people think of horseracing. Without doubt the Sport of Kings takes up a large part of the life and times of the Headquarters of flat racing. For many centuries the town has been an important stopping point on the main route from East Anglia to the west but without the sport of horseracing it is doubtful if Newmarket would have become more than an ordinary country market town.

The town straddles the border between two counties lying in what is almost an island of Suffolk intruding into Cambridgeshire. Approaching from the Cambridge direction the view takes in the High Street and an attractive glimpse of Warren Hill in the distance. To the north lie the flat fenlands, with Ely and its majestic cathedral a mere fourteen miles up the road. Southwards are the gentle rolling hills of East Cambridgeshire and West Suffolk. The real treasure of Newmarket is the Heath. Here are wide open spaces of ancient heathland to the east and west of the town, owned and managed by the Jockey Club but open to walkers for much of the time. It must present a tempting spectacle for would be developers but as long as horseracing continues as a national sport the Heath will remain hallowed ground.

The origins of the Newmarket we know today go back to King James I of England who found the open land around the town good for his sporting interests of hunting the hare and falconry. Horses inevitably came into the sport but it was not until Charles II's reign that horseracing really got under way. Charles of course was also fond of the ladies and had his favourite mistress Nell Gwynne installed conveniently close to his Newmarket royal residence at what is now Palace House. The site of her house in Palace Street is today one of the town's better known tourist attractions.

English Kings and Queens, with few exceptions, have continued to this day to be attracted by the racing scene and the Royal patronage has in turn brought in the wealthy lovers of the turf. Signs of Newmarket's past and present wealth may be seen in the many fine and historic buildings around the town. Inevitably the town also became a centre for less noble sports such as cock fighting and gambling and many alehouses sprang up where money changed hands. Some of the really old inns like The Bushel, The Bull, The Crown and the Waggon and Horses still thrive today.

The three-quarters of a mile long High Street divides the town roughly into two, its ends marked by the Cooper Memorial and the Clock Tower. Everywhere in Newmarket one meets evidence of racing, with horses taking priority over cars. Racehorses are highly valuable and well cared for animals that even have their own swimming pool for exercising. Approaching the town by road in the morning one is likely to be held up by long strings of sleek racehorses with their stable lad and lassie riders as they cross the road on their way to or from the gallops on the Heath. Many famous racing stables are dotted around the town, and studs and racing stables extend to the outlying villages. Almost without exception the racing premises are beautifully maintained - racehorses deserve the very best in accommodation. In the town there are businesses devoted to bookmakers, farriers, saddlery and horse requisites. High quality shops offer apparel and jewellery to go with the racing scene. The imposing Jockey Club building and the National Horseracing museum are centrally placed in the High Street, the National Stud is two miles along the Cambridge Road near the July Racecourse entrance.

Walking along the High Street on Tuesday or Saturday market days one is aware of a lively, bustling town. The many people you meet who by stature or attire mark them as connected with horse racing are a constant reminder of the core business of Newmarket as they mingle with local shoppers and country folk from the villages. In the evenings another kind of liveliness takes over as young people from a wide area are drawn to the town as if by a magnet by the two chief night-clubs.

On the big race days the town becomes even busier with horse transporters and expensive cars thronging the High Street. Racing is an international sport, with wealthy foreign owners investing huge amounts of money into the district. The meetings take place from mid-April until early November, beginning on the Rowley Mile Course then moving to the July Course from late June to August, finally ending the season back on the Rowley Mile. A popular innovation in recent years has been the holding of evening meetings on the July Course and to include a cabaret as part of the entertainment. Huge sums change hands too at Tattersalls Sales, held on various dates from April to December, with the main auctions in October and November. Here the bidding is traditionally in guineas, running into seven figures for highly rated yearlings.

What else can the town offer the visitor? Shops and hotels there are aplenty, with the imposing building of the Rutland Arms Hotel towards the eastern end of the High Street. Just behind the Rutland, Palace House is now the Tourist Information Centre and this perhaps should be the first port of call. From the entrances in The Avenue or in Park Paddocks Road at the top end of Queensberry Road, visit Tattersalls, where the visitor can walk through the famous Park Paddocks without charge. Take a walk along elegant Bury Road to see the many fine houses and more stables. From the Clock Tower follow the Moulton Road to Warren Hill, the best place to see horses exercising in the morning and to get a panoramic view of the town. Drive along the beautiful tree-lined Duchess Drive to Saxon Street and return by Wood Ditton and Stetchworth to get a taste of the quiet countryside bordering the town. Walk the Devil's Ditch, the Anglo-Saxon earthworks rich in chalk loving wild flowers, which is intersected by the Cambridge Road quite near to the National Stud.

There is no doubt that Newmarket has a blend of features giving it a unique character that has survived the changes in society that have overwhelmed some towns. The following pages set out to illustrate some of the scenes and highlights that make Newmarket the attractive place that it is to visit today, whatever your interest.

The Jockey Club owns the Heath and is generous in allowing public access for walkers on these wide-open spaces. Few restrictions are imposed but before 1 p.m. some sections are closed to walkers while on others dog owners are required to keep their pets on a lead by which time most of the horses have finished their morning exercise. The picture shows part of the Heath known as Cambridge Hill lying between Cambridge Road and the private road leading to the Rowley Mile racecourse.

These cottages facing the Links golf-course and owned by the Jockey Club were once the grandstands for an old steeplechase course built by racing personality and landowner Col. Harry McCalmont at the end of the 19th century. Steeplechasing had a brief period of popularity but the Newmarket trainers preferred flat racing. After the Colonel died in 1902 the Jockey Club bought the buildings and eventually converted them to cottages.

The Links Golf Club is reached from Cambridge Road about a mile from the town centre. The course is within the perimeter of the old steeplechase course and runs up to the Devil's Ditch. The picture shows the clubhouse. (Map point 7)

Two tees of the Links Golf-course are on the bank of the Devil's Ditch which forms the western boundary of the club's grounds. Here a golfer drives off from the par four 15th

Queensberry House at the western end of High Street is the home of the British Bloodstock Agency. The present building built in 1898 by the highly regarded architect Col. R W Edis replaced the original one owned by the Marquis of Queensberry. (Map point 10)

3

Many past personalities in the world of racing are buried in Newmarket's Cemetery at the western end of High Street, none more famous than Fred Archer the brilliant jockey whose life ended at the age of 29 after a series of personal tragedies. (Map point 9)

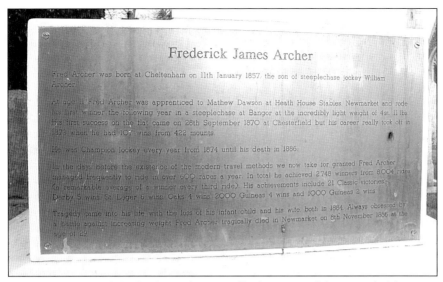

The plaque on Fred Archer's tombstone tells the story of the remarkable career of the jockey who started riding when only eleven. He was champion jockey from 1874 until 1886 despite a constant battle to control his weight which took a toll on his health. Having lost both his infant son and his wife in 1884 he took his own life two years later.

The White Lion near the western end of High Street was built in the nineteen thirties on the site of a very old inn of the same name. What appear to have once been stables remain at the rear. Today the pub has a restaurant and offers bed & breakfast accommodation.

These distinguished buildings on the north side of the western end of High Street lead towards the old and disused Queensberry Stables. The railings in the foreground mark the end of The Terrace.

This building in High Street started life as The Doric cinema in 1937 but with the decline in cinema attendance it closed in the nineteen seventies. It now has a new life as The Orange House, a spacious pub. The building also houses Pacino's Wine Bar and Surfers' Paradise Internet Café while at the rear is De Niro's Nite Cub, a popular venue for the young.

Some of Newmarket's most elegant Georgian houses are to be seen on The Terrace, the raised access roadway running beside High Street near its western end. Once the homes of wealthy racing personalities, including the flamboyant Lord Lonsdale, they are now mainly in use for business purposes.

7

Built in 1914 on land donated by Sir Ernest Cassel, the King Edward VII Memorial Hall has filled many roles. Today it serves as a meeting room and hosts an indoor craft market and the offices of the Newmarket Town Council. (Map point 13)

The Memorial Hall must have been very substantially built as it withstood a very near miss when the town was bombed in February 1941. Traces of the damage on the front of the building can still be seen.

One of the great names in racing history - Sidney, Earl of Godolphin became famous as a patron of the turf and an influential supporter of the monarchy from Charles II to the reign of Queen Anne. This house on the corner of High Street and The Avenue was built in the early 18th century as the home of the Godolphin family. Today the name is kept alive as the title of the international racing organisation owned by the Al-Maktoum family.

Ye Olde Scotch Tea Rooms probably formed part of the early 18th century Godolphin House. The rooms include a bakery as well a meeting place for refreshments. An unusual feature is the enormous old open fireplace in the main refreshment area.

One of Newmarket's old established suppliers to the equine world, Gibson Saddlers Ltd in Sales Paddock Lane, produce specialist equipment on the premises. Here a craftsman is working on a leather saddle.

10

This example of the taxidermist's art in Gibson Saddlers Shop is the stuffed skin of Robert the Devil, the 1880 St Leger winner.

The Avenue runs from High Street towards the station. In the days when most racegoers travelled by train it would have been thronged with people and carriages on race days. Here we look along the tree-lined road towards High Street with the King Edward VII Memorial Hall visible at the end.

Coronation Court, another of the several Newmarket buildings designed by the noted architect Colonel R W Edis around the beginning of the 20th century. In the heyday of the railways most racegoers arrived by train and the Coronation Hotel was conveniently situated close by the station. It has now been converted to apartments.

Today The Avenue is a dignified road with some classic late Victorian/early Edwardian houses as well as the main entrance to Tattersalls Park Paddocks.

Tattersalls Park Paddocks main entrance in The Avenue. This family firm had its beginnings at Hyde Park Corner, London, in 1766 when Richard Tattersall founded a horse and hounds sales business. By 1870 Edmund Tattersall had acquired land at Newmarket and his son Edmund Somerville, 'Sommy' Tattersall (1863 – 1942) developed Park Paddocks as the firm's chief auction house. After World War II Tattersalls continued to grow in international standing under the chairmanship of Kenneth Watt. With Edmund Mahony, its present chairman, Tattersalls continues to be recognised as the greatest bloodstock agency in the world. (Map point 11)

Tattersalls stables where horses are cared for while on the premises.

Tattersalls Sale Ring is within this large building known as the Rotunda where the indoor auctions are conducted.

Here in Tattersalls Sale Ring bids are traditionally made in guineas under the skilful direction of the auctioneer. Sums paid for top class thoroughbreds can reach well into seven figures. In 1998 the yearling Abshurr obtained the record sum of three million guineas. The most important events are the autumn yearling sales held in October and November.

This elegant clock, just inside the Park Paddocks Road entrance to Tattersalls, once overlooked their original yard in Knightsbridge.

This large building on the corner of The Avenue and High Street was once a substantial mansion owned by Thomas Panton, 'Keeper of the King's Running Horses' to King George II. In the early 19th century it came into the ownership of William Crockford, a notorious gambler and local landowner. Divided into three premises after Crockford died, its central portion became the old Kingsway cinema, now the 'M' night-club.

The Jockey Club, headquarters of the governing body for horseracing, also owns most of the land around the town. Wealthy owners originally formed the club in 1750. The present building dates from 1937, the original having being destroyed by fire two years previously. It incorporates the National Horseracing Museum and a café at the rear. The Post Office next door was built to the same style after wartime bombing destroyed the original building. (Map point 15)

This fine bronze statue of the outstandingly successful stallion Hyperion (1930 - 1960) by John Skeaping stands at the front of the Jockey Club, in High Street.

High Street virtually divides the town into two halves and is usually busy with shoppers and traffic.

The National Horseracing Museum adjoins the Jockey Club and once formed part of the original building. As well as a fine collection of racing memorabilia, records and paintings it also has a shop and a café which has walls decorated with murals of racing personalities painted by local artist Jacquie Jones. In fine weather visitors can enjoy refreshments in the pretty little courtyard. (Map point 16)

The short and narrow Sun Lane connects High Street to All Saints' Church and includes this florally decorated old inn now called LTs, previously known as the Rising Sun

This building near the entrance to Market Street is believed to date from the time of rebuilding the area following the great fire of 1683 that ravaged this side of High Street. The shop, known as 'The Rocking Rabbit', sells quality speciality gifts, including arts and crafts.

Another historic Newmarket pub, The Bull in High Street. or the Black Bull, as it was originally known, appears on very early maps of the town and is believed to date from the 17th century. It is now a popular venue for the racing fraternity as well as visitors.

Once one of Newmarket's oldest pubs the Star inn on the corner of Sun Lane now serves as a wine shop. The building still retains some interesting and original architectural features both internally and externally.

Another of the old taverns in High Street, the Waggon & Horses continues as a popular meeting place near the Clock Tower end of High Street. The frontage of the building also has some interesting old features such as bow and sash windows

Jane's Dress Shop, as the building is known today, has had a long and chequered history. At the time of King Charles II a cock-pit existed in the cellar, this being the venue for one of his favourite diversions. During the 19th century it served as a theatre and then as the Town Hall. At the beginning of the 20th century films were shown here, and in 1907 a disastrous fire occurred when the projection equipment caught fire. From the ensuing panic deaths and many injuries resulted. Later in the 20th century the building became the Gas Company's showrooms. Today Jane's is a ladies' fashion shop of distinction and in the basement there is now a café and wine bar where the cock-fighting once took place.

The imposing frontage of the Rutland Arms Hotel dominates the eastern end of High Street. The present hotel was built in 1830 on the site of The Ram, an old coaching inn, parts of which still remain. Some evidence supports the legend that an underground tunnel once existed between the inn and nearby Nell Gwynne's House for the convenience of King Charles II's discreet visits while staying at the inn. The hotel acquired its name from the Duke of Rutland, once the Lord of the Manor for this side of Newmarket. The family crest and motto 'Pour y Parvenir' (to succeed) appears on the front gable of the hotel. The present day hotel management and staff aim to live up to that ideal in caring for their visitors and guests. (Map point 21)

The courtyard of The Rutland Hotel has many interesting features and makes an attractive entrance reminiscent of the old coaching days. Tables for light refreshments are set out in this area when the weather permits.

Lady Harriet Cooper had this fine monument erected in 1910 in memory of her husband Sir Daniel Cooper Bart., a popular racing figure and benefactor to the town. It marks the beginning of the High Street when arriving from Cambridge Road. (Map point 8)

The approach to the town from the higher ground at the Cambridge Road end of High Street gives a preview of the town centre and distant glimpses of Warren Hill on the other side of the town.

On Tuesdays and Saturdays, the stalls in the open part of the Rookery shopping area are busy with shoppers from the surrounding villages as well as townsfolk. The open market place adjoins the covered area of the Rookery and is in use as a car park on other days.

An historic Newmarket Inn with origins going back to 1577, The Crown in High Street is as popular today as ever.

Gibson Saddlers Ltd in Sales Paddock Lane at the top of Queensberry Road is the oldest established business in Newmarket providing this specialist craft to horseracing. In addition to leather riding tackle Gibsons supply a range of equine accessories. Pictured above are Directors Mike and Karl Butcher who run the business today.

Colourful racing colours or silks worn by jockeys to aid identification during racing are also made by Gibsons here seen displayed in their shop window.

The High Street on a market day in summer presents a lively and colourful scene. Local shoppers are joined by many from the surrounding villages. It is a friendly place where regular shoppers are always likely to meet somebody they know.

Tattersalls bloodstock agency is one of Newmarket's great institutions but the firm has not always been in Newmarket and they originally came from London. During World War II chairman Kenneth Watt brought 'The Fox' statue from Tattersalls' original Knightsbridge premises to Park Paddocks Newmarket to preserve it from German bombs. It has become a symbol of Tattersalls past and present.

Tattersalls Park Paddocks are beautifully set on ground rising from The Avenue. Here we look down towards the secondary entrance, with Cardigan Street just visible on the other side of The Avenue. (Map point 11)

Graham Snelling, curator of the National Horseracing Museum, holding a silk scarf sold to commemorate Blue Peter's Derby win in 1939. On the table, there is the winning jockey's saddle and part of a wing spar from a Spitfire wartime fighter plane. The connection with the Spitfire is that in 1941 the people of Newmarket donated £5,000 towards the cost of the plane and named it Blue Peter in honour of the horse. Having crashed in the Scottish Highlands in 1942, the plane remained buried in the peat until 1993 when a team of aircraft enthusiasts found the wreckage and recovered many parts including that shown in the picture. (Map point 16)

At the eastern end of the High Street, the Queen Victoria Jubilee Memorial Clock Tower proudly stands in the middle of a complex traffic roundabout. In recent years it was suggested that the clock be moved to make way for cars, but common sense prevailed and the monument retained its rightful place as the very symbol of Newmarket. (Map point 20)

As a child living in the heart of London Jacquie Jones had a passion for art. Her love of horses brought her to Newmarket where she had a brief spell as a work rider for trainer Henry Cecil, but by 1983 she was working as a professional artist. She is particularly known for her equestrian subjects and a flowing style that captures the essence and magic of horseracing. From her 'Nell Gwynne Studio' in Palace Street her works have sold all over the world. (Map point 22)

The picturesque village of Moulton is less than three miles east from Newmarket and is well worth a visit. The bridge seen here is one of the two 15th century bridges over the River Kennett and is only suitable for foot traffic and animals. The other bridge is featured in the black and white section of this book

To coincide with the new millennium, Newmarket Racecourses Trust embarked on a major improvement scheme which included demolishing the old grandstand and building this futuristic-looking new one at a cost of around £18,000,000. The Millennium Grandstand now provides racegoers with facilities where they can place their bets, dine and watch the racing in comfort. (Map point 4)

Side Hill is that part of the Heath bordering Old Station Road and leading up to the gallops on Warren Hill. It can be reached from the short residential Heath Road turning off Old Station Road. Although Heath Road is private, limited car parking is available by the entrance and this makes a good access point to the large expanse of Heath bounded by Bury Road and Warren Hill. Please note walkers are not allowed on these gallops before 1 pm. (Map point 33)

Simon Curtis is one of two brothers who run the old established Moulton Road business of Curtis Farriers.

In May each year this Judas tree (Cercis siliquastrum) in All Saints' churchyard puts on a splendid show. It was planted in the early nineteen-fifties and obviously is happy in its situation. Its blossoms have the unusual feature of growing directly out of the trunk and main branches as well as cloaking the canopy. Legend has it that Judas Iscariot hanged himself from one of these trees. (Map point 17)

The ancient chalk grassland of the Devil's Ditch supports a wide range of flowers including several species of orchid and other rare plants. It is at its richest from July to early autumn when this picture was taken. The July racecourse can be seen in the background.

Here in the Winners' Enclosure at the Rowley Mile Course winning horses are led in to receive the plaudits of their proud owners and trainers. (Map point 4)

The new facilities at the Rowley Mile include big screen viewing of the whole race.

Leaving Newmarket in a south-easterly direction towards Saxon Street the road gently climbs along the mile and a quarter of Duchess Drive. The Duke of Rutland planted the fine beeches bordering the road in the 18th century. He and the Duchess would have passed along here in their carriage from their Manor House in Cheveley Park on their way to Newmarket. Duchess Drive is beautiful at any time of the year but particularly in autumn when the leaves produce a riot of colour.

It's easy to pass through the little village of Snailwell two miles north of Newmarket without noticing the pretty St. Peter's Church with its rare flint-construction round tower. The Church dates from the 11th century but is now essentially as when restored in 1878. The large pool near the Church is the source of the River Snail. Both can be reached from the short no-through Church Lane.

The village of Wood Ditton lies three and a half miles to the south of Newmarket.

Its unique village sign by the crossroads was designed by local artist Chris Winch to commemorate the new millennium, and incorporates an armillary, an ancient device for telling the time from the sun, mounted over two crossed cartwheels at the base to signify the village's agricultural past and its dependence on the horse and cart. The figures of two men sawing timber recall the vast local woodlands from which the village name was partly derived.

The Rookery Shopping Centre was created in the nineteen seventies redevelopment of a very old and run-down area of Newmarket. Several streets disappeared completely but a few original buildings remain just outside the development area. This is the entrance to the covered shopping area from Market Street leading off from High Street. (Map point 19)

The main arcade of the popular Rookery Shopping Centre.

Reputed to be the oldest existing inn in Newmarket, The Bushel dates from the 17th century when cock-fighting and other disreputable pursuits used to be held here. Situated at the edge of the nineteen seventies Rookery shopping development, The Bushel stands in part of what used to be Drapery Row, most of which disappeared in the redevelopment.

High Street looking South West past the Rutland Arms.

Originally built for Charles II's horses, Palace House Stables, opposite and adjacent to Palace House, are the oldest in Newmarket. They have not been used since 1985 and now await a decision about their future.

Palace House stands on the site of the original Palace built for Charles II's visits to Newmarket. By Victorian times it had fallen into a poor state of repair and most of it was demolished. The Rothschild family turned it into a private residence in the early 20th century although very little of the original was retained. In the nineteen-nineties Forest Heath District Council, with the help of grants from English Heritage, took the building in hand and restored it to something like its original appearance. Today Palace House serves as the town's Tourist Information and Exhibition Centre. (Map point 23)

Palace Street runs from Rutland Hill and is separated from High Street by the Rutland Arms Hotel. On the left of this old street are the three cottages that made up Nell Gwynne's original house. Nell Gwynne had lowly beginnings but as a girl of considerable wit and some beauty she caught the eye of King Charles II. She became his friend and mistress and he installed her in the house close by his Palace. Legend has it that an underground passage ran to the house for the convenience of the King's visits but this has never been proven. At the bottom end of the street can be seen All Saints' Church. (Map point 22)

Plaques on the walls of cottages in Palace Street commemorate Nell Gwynne's association with Charles II. This one is inscribed with what were said to be his dying words to the Duke of York: "And let not poor Nelly starve".

Raye's Lane together with The Watercourse and The Rows is part of the horse walk crossing the town to and from the extensive Heath gallops to the west side of Newmarket. This route avoids roads and traffic except for the road crossings where horses have priority over cars.

Newmarket has a number of specialist trades and professions concerned with the equine world. Curtis Farriers in Moulton Road is the oldest established blacksmith in the district. Today brothers Simon and Mark Curtis carry on the family business started by their great-grandfather, Oliver Arthur Curtis.

St Mary's Church, standing at the edge of St Mary's Square, is believed to stand on the oldest church site in the town. Small parts of the present building date from the 15th century. (Map point 18)

Christchurch, the United Reformed Church at the side of Mill Hill on the north-eastern side of St Mary's Square, can be seen in the background, appearing just ahead of the leading horse.

Mill Hill, one of the road crossings for racehorses and riders on their way across the town between their stables in the Fordham Road area and the large expanse of gallops north of the Rowley Mile. The crossing links the horse walk known as The Watercourse with the one bordering St Mary's Square. This busy road leads to Exning, and motorists have to accept delays during the mornings when the horse traffic is at its peak. Mill Hill acquired its name from a windmill that once stood on top of the hill.

King's Theatre in Fitzroy Street started life as St Mary's Infants and Girls' School, but this closed down at the beginning of World War II when for a time the building served as a British Restaurant. A local benefactor, Capt. King, later bought and donated it to the town's Dramatic Society. It is still known as King's Theatre and the group called 'The Nomads' stage a variety of productions here.

This building in Exning Road was originally part of the Newmarket Union Workhouse, a refuge for tramps and paupers. Converted into the White Lodge Emergency Medical Services Hospital early in World War II it later became Newmarket General Hospital. Now the original buildings have been completely redeveloped into high-grade private houses and flats. The new hospital buildings adjoin them. (Map point 36)

The town's memorial to those who died in the two world wars stands in a small park garden close by the Clock Tower and on the edge of The Severals. (Map point 25)

Boyce House in Sackville Street (off the Moulton Road) was built in the late
19th century on the site of a much older house. The road used to be called
Shagbag Alley after the name of the hood used to cover the heads of fighting
cocks. A sunken area in the rear garden of the present house provides evidence
that this was the site of one of Newmarket's cock-pits

Cleveland House in Old Station Road and not far from the Clock Tower is
arguably one of the finest proportioned buildings in the town. The Duke of
Cleveland extensively rebuilt it in the early 19th century for his favourite
jockey, Sam Chifney junior. Today the building serves as offices. (Map point
31)

This building on the corner of Old Station Road and Vicarage Road used to be the old Rous Hospital, built in 1879 in memory of the well known Victorian patron of the turf Admiral Rous. The hospital served the local community well and many people have affectionate memories of the dedicated care provided by the staff. With the move towards larger and more centralised hospital services it closed in the early nineteen sixties and was eventually converted to flats for the elderly, a role that continues today. (Map point 24)

Rous Road, just off High Street quite near to the Clock Tower, includes these late 19th century terraced houses with what appears to be Dutch influence.

Early morning – Side Hill gallops as seen from Old Station Road. (Map point 3)

Warren Hill is one of best parts of the Heath to watch horses during their morning training exercises, although for safety reasons the public are required to confine themselves to the Moulton Road viewing areas before 1 p.m. This is also a good place to obtain a panoramic view of Newmarket and the distant Fenlands beyond. (Map point 32)

As Bury Road nears the Clock Tower Roundabout it passes the open space of the Severals. Here the morning traffic is likely to be held up by long strings of racehorses crossing the road.

The open grass area of the Severals lies between Fordham Road and Bury Road, near to their beginning by Clock Tower roundabout. Very busy in the morning with horses crossing from the various nearby stables, the Severals also provides an open space for some of the town's outdoor events. (Map point 26)

The Severals is not exclusively taken over by horses and its open space is used for recreational activities such as this Sunday morning game of football.

The Warren Hill horse walk used by horses returning from exercise, with Newmarket town spread out below

This shows the entrance to one of Newmarket's oldest racing stables, Heath House Stables Moulton Road, near the foot of Warren Hill. Heath House has a long history of training successful thoroughbreds and was owned by one of the great patrons and founders of horseracing, Tregonwell Frampton, who died in 1727. Fred Archer was apprenticed to these stables at age eleven and when success came he had a house on the premises. Archer always suffered from a weight problem and one of his remedies was to use a kind of crude Turkish bath installed at the stables. Remaining parts of it are still referred to as 'Fred Archer's Sweat Box'. On the opposite side of Moulton Road is Osborne House Stables. Both stables come under the direction of trainer Sir Mark Prescott.

The mile long stretch of Bury Road makes a dignified entry to the town from the east and is bordered by many fine 19th century houses most of them having been connected with racing for at least part of their existence. Several famous racing stables are also located here including Godolphin, Bedford House, Freemason Lodge, Sefton Lodge and Carlburg.

Built in 1886 by Caroline Agnes, Duchess of Montrose, as a memorial to her second husband, St Agnes Church in Bury Road has a Lych Gate entrance and a lavish interior. (Map point 35)

Amberley in Bury Road must surely be a contender for the prettiest house in Newmarket, although these days it is divided into flats.

Standing in three acres of its own grounds on the north side of Bury Road, Bedford Lodge Hotel is a combination of old and new as it is based on the old Georgian Hunting Lodge built for the Duke of Bedford in the late 18th century. After World War II it was converted for use as a hotel. Today the complex forms a large and stylish hotel with excellent conference and banqueting facilities. (Map point 27)

The Jockey Club owns extensive Heath gallops both to the west and east of the town. Nearing Newmarket from the Bury St Edmunds or Norwich direction the roads pass across this area of Heath, part of which is known as the Limekilns; lime was quarried in this area.

The tree lined avenue leading to the Rowley Mile Course and Grandstand is private but the Jockey Club allow public access. The picture shows it busy with traffic on a race day. (Map point 6)

The Devil's Ditch (or Dyke) stretches seven miles from Wood Ditton in the south to Reach in the north. Built in Anglo-Saxon times some 1450 years ago, it was intended to deter invaders from Romanised Britain in the west from entering the Anglo-Saxon Kingdoms in East Anglia. The section pictured here runs parallel with the July Racecourse and is open in character, giving good views of the Heath and of racing in progress. Further south the Ditch becomes increasingly wooded.

South of the Cambridge Road gap the Devil's Ditch path is flanked by these pine trees before coming to the more open part bordering the Links Golf Course.

This propeller blade came from a wartime Wellington bomber operating from the Heath which crashed in 1941 near the town of Wisbech. It now stands close to the entrance to the Members' Enclosure at the Rowley Mile racecourse as a memorial to No 99 Squadron based here from September 1939 to March 1941. The plaque on the wall is a memorial to the many airmen who lost their lives.

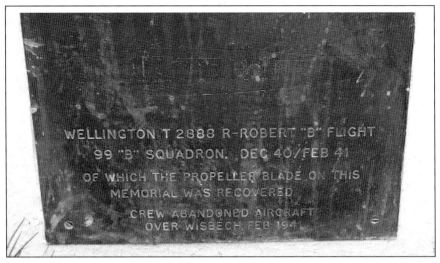

The plaque on the propeller plinth.

Brigadier Gerard the famous classic winner (1964 – 1989) still graces the Rowley Mile Paddock

The bronze of Eclipse by John Osborne can be seen in the Rowley Mile racecourse enclosure. One of the great ancestors of today's thoroughbred horses, Eclipse was bred by the Duke of Cumberland in 1764 and was named after the great solar eclipse of that year. It was said of the horse that it put all others in the shade.

Excitement mounts as the runners near the finish post on the famous Rowley Mile Racecourse, named after King Charles II's favourite horse 'Old Rowley'.

A popular introduction to the racing calendar during the summer months has been the evening meetings on the July Course. The racing is usually followed by an outdoor cabaret to round off the evening, and this has attracted many young people who are new to the racing scene. (Map point 3)

The Parade Ring inside the Rowley Mile enclosure where horses are walked before races, giving the punters an opportunity to judge their condition.

There are two ways of placing bets on the racecourse, by using the official betting agency 'the Tote' or by doing business with one of the individual bookmakers where one might get better odds. Here the bookmakers are in action while on the course a racehorse canters towards the starting gates.

This statue of Chamossaire (1942 – 1964) by John Skeaping stands on the left side of the Snailwell Road just before reaching the village. The stallion won the St Leger and also sired several classic race winners.

Chippenham Junction, just a mile north-east of Newmarket, is where the line from Bury St. Edmunds branches two ways. To the left it passes through Warren Hill tunnel to Newmarket and then on to Cambridge and London. To the right it runs to Ely and the north. A short stretch of line once linked the two branches but it is no longer possible to go by rail directly from Newmarket to Ely and passengers have to change trains at Cambridge.

Continuous streams of traffic flow along the A14 Newmarket bypass, the main route between East Anglia and the Midlands. Up to the nineteen seventies the route went through Newmarket's High Street, which these days, nevertheless, is often busier than before the bypass was built.

The village of Chippenham lies three miles north of Newmarket but is still within the horseracing orbit. Chippenham Hall was once the home of the Tharp family, Lords of the Manor in the 19th and early 20th century. It is still a private residence but the magnificent gardens are usually opened to the public three times a year under the National Gardens Scheme. A grand gateway, a few hundred yards from the end of Bury Road, guards the entrance to a two mile long private drive to the Hall. (Gateway map point 30)

For many years travellers along the B1506 road from Newmarket to Kentford have pondered on the story of the grave by the crossroads, about a mile before the village. It is known to have been there for at least a hundred years. One legend is that a gypsy boy was charged with watching a flock of sheep but he fell asleep and the flock wandered off. Filled with remorse, he hanged himself. Another version is that an orphan boy was wrongly accused of stealing a sheep. Always there are flowers on the grave said to be placed there by passing gypsy folk. Some believe that the colours of the flowers can predict the colours of the winning jockey at Newmarket's big races. The wooden cross is a comparatively recent addition to the grave and bears the simple inscription 'Joseph the unknown gypsy boy'.

This is the magnificent 15th century Packhorse Bridge at Moulton, the attractive village three miles east of Newmarket. It crosses the little river Kennett that in recent years is much diminished in flow and seldom liable to flood. Road traffic uses the ford crossing alongside the bridge.

70

This imposing gateway is the Duchess Drive entrance to the near 1000 acres of Cheveley Park Stud, one of the oldest in the country. Many famous horses have been associated with it, including the stallion Isinglass, put to stud in 1896 after achieving 11 victories from 12 starts. Today Cheveley Park continues to produce successful thoroughbreds.

The horse and rider are about to leave the top end of Duchess Drive where the road passes through farmland before reaching the hamlet of Saxon Street.

The origins of St Martin's Church Exning reputedly go back to the arrival of Christianity in the district around the 7th century. Exning existed as a village and market place long before trade moved two miles south to the route of the Icknield Way and a "new market" opened, hence the name of the present town.

The tall octagonal tower of the Church of St Mary the Virgin at Wood Ditton
distinguishes this old parish church. Its origins probably go back to the 12th
century, although like most churches it has been rebuilt or added to over the
years. It stands on high ground about three miles south of Newmarket and
three quarters of a mile from the main centre of the village at Ditton Green.
In the tower a fine set of five bells ring out for special services and at the
usual practice on Tuesday evenings.

73

This little stream running beside Ducks Lane in Exning is a favourite place for watching and feeding the ducks. The village also has a Swan Lane but the two geese don't seem to mind the absence of a Goose Lane.

Stetchworth is a pleasant village standing on rising ground in a rural setting. Situated only three miles from Newmarket, it is much influenced by horseracing with studs and grazing paddocks within the parish. Famous personalities in the racing world have lived here, including the Earl of Ellesmere, the Duke of Sutherland, Steve Cauthen and at the present time Frankie Dettori. The picture shows the War Memorial and Millennium Sign on the little village green at the beginning of Church Lane. St Peter's Church and the entrance to Stetchworth Park House are near the end of Church Lane.

These attractive cottages in Wood Ditton Road Newmarket were built by the Duke of Rutland in 1864 when he was Lord of the Manor of the parish of Wood Ditton in which they lie. Motorists seldom give them a glance as they slow for the 30 mph speed limit on approaching the outskirts of the town.

The National Stud started its existence in Ireland but moved to the present location in 1963. An anonymous quotation once described the aims of the National Stud - 'Breed the best to the best and hope for the best'. Certainly over the years many successful horses have been bred here, perhaps the greatest stallion being Mill Reef in 1968. The picture shows the entrance from the private road leading to the July Racecourse. Guided tours are available from March to September. (Map point 2)

The Newmarket Stallion on the Cambridge Road roundabout. (Map point 1)

NEWMARKET TOWN PLAN

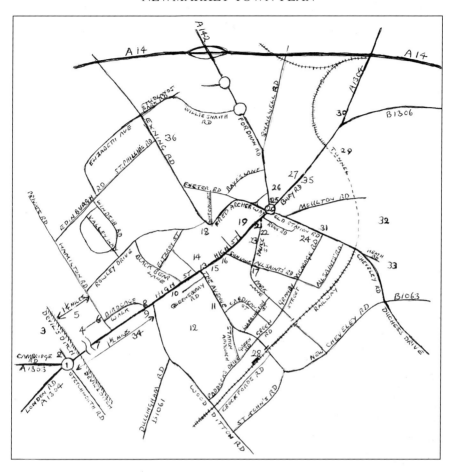

Key to Places of Interest

1 Newmarket Stallion Statue on London Road Roundabout
2 National Stud and entrance to July Racecourse
3 July Racecourse and Grandstands
4 Millennium Grandstand and Rowley Mile Racecourse
5 Heath Gallops
6 Entrance to Rowley Mile Racecourse
7 Links Golf-club
8 Daniel Cooper Memorial
9 Newmarket Town Cemetery
10 Queensberry House
11 Tattersalls Entrance in The Avenue
12 Tattersalls Park Paddocks
13 King Edward VII Memorial Hall
14 King Edward VII Memorial Gardens
15 Post Office, Jockey Club
16 National Horse Racing Museum
17 All Saints' Church
18 St Mary's Square and Church
19 Rookery Shopping Centre
20 Clock Tower Roundabout
21 Rutland Arms Hotel
22 Nell Gwynne's House
23 Palace House – Tourist Information Centre
24 Rous Court (Former Hospital)
25 War Memorial and Garden
26 The Severals
27 Bedford Lodge Hotel
28 Rail Station
29 Long Hill gallops
30 Chippenham Park Entrance (private)
31 Cleveland House
32 Warren Hill
33 Side Hill Gallops
34 The Links Golf Club
35 St Agnes Church
36 Newmarket General Hospital